Table of Contents

1. Love Jokes

Valentines Day Jokes Book for Kids

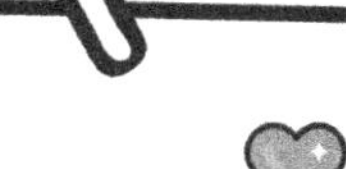 Welcome, Giggle Champion! 💖

Hey there, Valentine! 

You just opened a book that's bursting with jokes, laughter, and love! But before we dive in, here's a little riddle to get you started:

What did one light bulb say to the other on Valentine's Day?

💡 "I love you watts and watts!"

Pretty bright, huh? 😄 Get ready to tickle your funny bone, warm your heart, and share some giggles with everyone you love. Flip the page, and let the laughs begin!

PS: Don't forget - you're awesome and someone thinks you're "egg-cellent!" 🐣

Welcome to The Valentines Day Jokes Book for Kids! Packed with over 400 silly, sweet, and laugh-out-loud jokes, this book is perfect for kids, teens, and families who love to share smiles and spread love. Whether you're looking for clever puns, funny riddles, or heartwarming giggles, you'll find something here for every Valentine's moment.

From school Valentine exchanges to family celebrations, these jokes are sure to make your day extra special. So grab your favorite candy, gather your loved ones, and get ready to laugh your heart out - because love and laughter are the best gifts of all!

Let the fun begin!

Why did the banana go out with the prune? Because it couldn't find a date!

What do you call two birds in love? Tweethearts!

Why do melons always get married? Because they cantaloupe!

What did one volcano say to the other? I lava you!

Why did the phone propose? With a ring!

What do you call a very small Valentine? A valen-tiny!

How did the farmer find love? He planted a kiss!

What's a heart's favorite song? "Beats Forever!"

Why did the star fall in love? It found its match in the sky!

What's a ghost's Valentine wish? A haunting love!

Why was the magnet so romantic? It was drawn to everyone!

What's a couple's favorite treat? Love-letters!

Why did the lovebirds build a nest together? They were "tweet" on each other!

Why was the diary full on Valentine's Day? It kept writing love stories!

What did the bracelet say to the necklace? I love hanging around with you!

Why did the chef fall in love with a recipe? It was love at first bite!

What's Cupid's favorite candy? Heart-pops!

What do you call a Valentine's card for a spider? Web of love!

Why was the heart full of glitter? It wanted to sparkle with love!

Why did the artist fall in love with their painting? It was a masterpiece of the heart!

2. Laughter Jokes

What's a laughing heart's favorite snack? Chuckle-chip cookies!

Why do bees love Valentine's Day? They like to buzz with joy!

What do you call a really funny Valentine's card? A joke-of-all-hearts!

Why did Cupid fail at stand-up comedy? His punchlines were too arrow-dynamic!

What do chocolates tell jokes about? Sweet nothings!

Why do jokes bring hearts closer? They tickle their love strings!

Why did the teddy bear join the laughter club? It couldn't bear the sadness!

Why are comedians so popular on Valentine's Day? They know how to tickle your heart!

Why did the joke date the pun? It found it irresistible!

What's Cupid's favorite joke? "I bow to your humor!"

What do you call a joke you tell your crush? A heart-felt pun!

Why did the love letter giggle? It had ticklish words!

What do laugh emojis send for Valentine's Day? Giggle-grams!

Why did the lovebird love jokes? It wanted to chirp with joy!

What do roses tell each other? "We're blooming funny together!"

Why do jokes always win at love games? They're full of charm!

What's the funniest Valentine's Day gift? A tickle-box!

Why do Valentine's jokes never break hearts? They're delivered with love!

What do comedians call their Valentine's Day? The giggle-fest!

Why do balloons love jokes? They love being lifted!

3. Family Jokes

Why did Dad buy flowers on Valentine's Day? To plant some smiles at home!

What's Nana's favorite Valentine's dessert? Love-ly pie!

Why did Grandpa knit a sweater for Valentine's Day? To wrap Nana in love!

What do siblings exchange on Valentine's Day? Punny jokes and candy!

Why did Mom bake heart-shaped cookies? To fill everyone with love!

What did Grandpa say to Grandma? "You've aged like fine love!"

Why did the brother give his sister candy hearts? She was a sweet part of his life!

What did the family dog say on Valentine's Day? "I woof you!"

Why did the grandparents take a walk on Valentine's Day? To stroll down memory lane!

Why did the baby giggle on Valentine's Day? It was all baby love!

What did Dad say about his Valentine card? "It's pun-tastic!"

Why did the family decorate the house? To spread heartwarming joy!

Why did the little brother draw a big heart? To show he loved his family BIG!

What did Mom say to the kids? "You're the chocolate to my heart!"

Why did the sister love Valentine's Day? She got glittery cards!

Why did the family play board games? They wanted to share the love!

Why did Grandma tell a Valentine's joke? To tickle everyone's heartstrings!

What's a family's favorite Valentine game? Hide-and-love!

Why did the parents love their kids' Valentine cards? They were made with heart!

What's the best Valentine gift for Dad? A mug that says "World's Sweetest Heart!"

4. Humor Jokes

Why did the scarecrow win a Valentine's Day contest? Because he was outstanding in his field of love!

What do you call a Valentine's joke that falls flat? A broken heart!

Why do chocolates always win arguments? Because they're so sweet!

What do clouds give each other on Valentine's Day? Rainbows of love!

What's the funniest gift to give your Valentine? A pun-in-a-box!

Why did the cookie write a love letter? It was crumbling with feelings!

What's the best Valentine's Day joke for a car? "You auto be mine!"

Why did the bow tie go to the Valentine's party? It wanted to look tie-rific!

What did the strawberry say to the chocolate? "We're berry sweet together!"

Why did the calendar bring a flower? It wanted to mark the date with love!

What's the best joke to tell Cupid? "You really nailed it with your bow!"

Why did the chicken bring chocolates? To egg-spress its love!

What's a chef's favorite Valentine pun? "You're the salt to my pepper!"

Why do chocolates write the best jokes? They have layers of sweetness!

Why was the Valentine's Day card so funny? It had a lot of pun-ch lines!

Why did the broom send a Valentine? It swept someone off their feet!

What did the lightbulb say to its Valentine? "You brighten up my life!"

Why did the squirrel propose? It went nuts over its Valentine!

What's a snowman's favorite Valentine's gift? A warm hug!

Why do magnets make good Valentines? Because they're so attractive!

5. Games Jokes

Why did the deck of cards throw a Valentine's Day party? It was a full house of love!

What's a Valentine's favorite sport? Love-ball!

Why did the puzzle fall in love? It found its missing piece!

What's Cupid's favorite board game? Loveopoly!

Why did the dice propose? It rolled into love!

What's a balloon's favorite game on Valentine's Day? Heart pop!

Why did the kite fall in love? It was carried away by the wind!

What's the most romantic card game? Hearts!

Why did the marbles pair up on Valentine's Day? They didn't want to lose their connection!

What's a video gamer's favorite Valentine line? "You leveled up my heart!"

Why did the dominoes write love letters? They wanted to fall for each other!

What's the best Valentine's game for kids? Pin the heart on Cupid!

Why did the spinner get nervous on Valentine's Day? It had to turn on the charm!

What did the dice say to the playing cards? "You're my perfect match!"

Why do teddy bears make great prizes for Valentine's Day games? They're huggable!

What's a yo-yo's Valentine wish? To come back into someone's life!

Why did the kids love the Valentine's treasure hunt? It was full of heart!

What did the video game controller say to its Valentine? "You've got me wired!"

Why did the chess pieces fall in love? They had great moves!

What's the most romantic sport? Archery—it's all about Cupid's aim!

6. Food Jokes

Why was the chocolate feeling confident? It was wrapped in love!

What's a pizza's favorite Valentine's card? "You've stolen a pizza my heart!"

Why did the cake write a poem? It wanted to be sweet!

What did the popcorn say to the butter? "You make my heart pop!"

Why did the bread fall in love? It found the perfect jam!

What's a fruit's favorite Valentine line? "You're grape to me!"

Why was the candy heart so popular? It was full of sugar and spice!

What's a hamburger's Valentine wish? "Let's ketchup on love!"

Why did the carrot give roses? To root for love!

What's an ice cream's favorite Valentine line? "You're the cherry on top!"

Why did the donut write a Valentine? It had a hole lotta love!

What's a cupcake's favorite Valentine message? "You're frosting on my heart!"

Why did the pancake propose? It flipped over someone special!

What's the best Valentine for a chef? "You're the zest of my life!"

Why did the milkshake write a love note? It was whipped with love!

What did the cookie tell the brownie? "We're sweet together!"

What's a watermelon's Valentine wish? "You're one in a melon!"

Why did the coffee bring flowers? It wanted to espresso its love!

What's the best Valentine for a baker? A heart full of dough!

Why did the ice cube love Valentine's Day? It was melting with love!

7.School Jokes

Why did the math book send a Valentine? It wanted to show its love for solving problems!

What's a pencil's favorite Valentine message? "You're write for me!"

Why did the eraser bring flowers? It wanted to make a clean start!

What's a student's favorite Valentine's Day project? Crafting heart-filled cards!

Why did the teacher love Valentine's Day? She had a class full of sweethearts!

Why did the crayons get together on Valentine's Day? They wanted to draw love!

What did the glue say to the scissors? "You make my heart stick!"

Why did the notebook blush? It saw the love note!

What's the most romantic school supply? The stapler—it's always connecting hearts!

What did the ruler say to the Valentine? "You measure up perfectly!"

Why did the chalk feel special? Someone drew their heart with it!

What's the best Valentine's Day subject? History—learning about Cupid's past!

Why did the paper clip fall in love? It was hooked on someone!

What's a library's Valentine wish? "Let's check each other out!"

Why was the school desk happy on Valentine's Day? It was covered in love notes!

What's Cupid's favorite classroom? Art class—it's full of creativity!

Why did the back-to-school supplies get excited? Valentine's Day added a spark of love!

What did the bookmark say to the book? "You're my place in the world!"

Why do kids love Valentine's Day at school? Because it's full of sweet treats and cards!

What did the chalkboard write? "You've drawn my heart!"

8.Gifts Jokes

Why did the teddy bear refuse another Valentine? It was already stuffed with love!

What's the most romantic gift for a chef? A spice rack full of love!

Why did the box of chocolates feel proud? It was filled with sweet

What's a cat's favorite Valentine gift? A "purr-fect" box of treats!

Why did the gift card feel loved? It had a heartfelt message!

What's the best Valentine gift for a baker? A dozen "sweet"

Why did the scarf make a great gift? It wrapped up love perfectly!

What's the most musical Valentine gift? A love song playlist!

Why did the rose bouquet blush? It was picked with love!

What did the gift box say? "You've unwrapped my heart!"

What's a snowman's favorite gift? A warm Valentine hug!

Why did the puppy make the best Valentine's gift? It gave unconditional love!

What's the most magical Valentine gift? A heart-shaped wand!

Why did the balloon get excited? It was floating with love!

What's a bird's favorite Valentine gift? A nest filled with heart-shaped twigs!

Why was the heart necklace special? It kept love close!

What's a poet's favorite Valentine gift? A notebook full of love poems!

Why do chocolates make the best gifts? They melt hearts!

What's the sweetest gift to share? A smile!

Why do homemade Valentine gifts mean so much? They're made with love!

9.Knock-Knock Jokes

Knock, knock.
Who's there?
Heart.
Heart who?
Heart you glad it's Valentine's Day?

Knock, knock.
Who's there?
Olive.
Olive who?
Olive you so much!

Knock, knock.
Who's there?
Candy.
Candy who?
Candy you feel the love in the air?

Knock, knock.
Who's there?
Cupid.
Cupid who?
Cupid sending love your way!

Knock, knock.
Who's there?
Bee.
Bee who?
Bee mine, Valentine!

Knock, knock.
Who's there?
Rose.
Rose who?
Rose you a Valentine's Day card!

Knock, knock.
Who's there?
Bunny.
Bunny who?
Bunny one as sweet as you?

Knock, knock.
Who's there?
Teddy.
Teddy who?
Teddy bear loves you!

Knock, knock.
Who's there?
Love.
Love who?
Love to share some chocolate!

Knock, knock.
Who's there?
Valentine.
Valentine who?
Valentine you'll be mine!

Knock, knock.
Who's there?
Sweets.
Sweets who?
Sweets the best Valentine ever!

Knock, knock.
Who's there?
Glow.
Glow who?
Glow Valentine, you light up my heart!

Knock, knock.
Who's there?
Charm.
Charm who?
Charm glad we're friends!

Knock, knock.
Who's there?
Cheer.
Cheer who?
Cheer my Valentine forever!

Knock, knock.
Who's there?
Flower.
Flower who?
Flower you my Valentine?

Knock, knock.
Who's there?
Heart.
Heart who?
Heart you excited for Valentine's?

Knock, knock.
Who's there?
Hope.
Hope who?
Hope you'll be my Valentine!

Knock, knock.
Who's there?
Hug.
Hug who?
Hug you tightly, Valentine!

Knock, knock.
Who's there?
Sprinkles.
Sprinkles who?
Sprinkles on our love story!

Knock, knock.
Who's there?
Wish.
Wish who?
Wish you a Happy Valentine's!

10. Party Jokes

Why did the party balloons love Valentine's Day? They got to float with happiness!

What's a cupcake's favorite party activity? Spreading frosting love!

Why was the Valentine's party so lively? Love was in the air!

What's a pizza's favorite party theme? "You've stolen a pizza my heart!"

Why did the popcorn enjoy the party? It was popping with excitement!

What's Cupid's favorite party music? Love songs on repeat!

Why do hearts love dancing at parties? They beat to the rhythm of love!

What's a snowman's Valentine's party game? Melt tag!

Why did the kids love the Valentine's photo booth? It captured heartwarming memories!

What's a candy heart's party anthem? "Sweet Love!"

Why did the Valentine's piñata feel special? It was filled with love!

What's the most romantic party favor? A heartfelt thank-you card!

Why did the roses decorate the party? To add blooming beauty!

What's the best game at a Valentine's party? Heart scavenger hunt!

Why do chocolates love party games? They're sweet winners!

What's a teddy bear's favorite Valentine's party activity? Hugs all around!

Why did the Valentine's party invite the crayons? To color the day with love!

What's a heart's favorite Valentine's party game? Musical chairs with love!

Why did the cookies enjoy the Valentine's Day party? They were freshly baked with love!

What's the best party dessert? Heart-shaped brownies!

11. Sweet Treats Jokes

Why did the candy heart write a song? It wanted to express its sweet feelings!

What's a donut's Valentine wish? "I'm sweet on you!"

Why did the ice cream cone blush? It was melting with love!

What's a cookie's favorite Valentine line? "You're one smart cookie!"

Why do cakes love Valentine's Day? They get to show their layers of love!

What's the best Valentine's treat? A smile served with chocolate!

Why do chocolate bars make great Valentines? They always break hearts sweetly!

Why did the pie write a love letter? It had fillings for someone special!

What's a fruit's favorite Valentine line? "You're my main squeeze!"

Why did the milkshake feel proud? It had the sweetest toppings!

What's the best Valentine dessert? Love cupcakes with sprinkles of joy!

Why do kids love Valentine's treats? They're made with extra hugs!

Why did the lollipop smile? It was a sucker for love!

What's a candy cane's favorite Valentine line? "You're sweet and twisted!"

Why did the cookie crumble on Valentine's Day? It was overwhelmed with love!

What's a marshmallow's Valentine wish? "You melt my heart!"

Why did the brownie bring flowers? To spread sweetness!

What's the most romantic ice cream flavor? Chocolate "heart swirl!"

Why did the candy heart dance? It was sugar-high on love!

What's a pie's favorite Valentine's Day joke? "You're filling my heart!"

12.Heart Jokes

Why did the heart write a poem? It was bursting with love!

What's a heart's favorite Valentine's Day decoration? Love lights!

Why did the heart get excited? It skipped a beat for someone special!

What's a heart's favorite treat? Chocolate kisses!

Why was the heart so creative? It loved thinking outside the box!

What's the heart's favorite emoji? ❤ !

Why did the heart blush? It was full of love!

What's a heart's favorite holiday? Valentine's Day!

Why did the heart join a band? It had great rhythm!

What's a heart's favorite sound? The beat of love!

Why was the heart so confident? It was full of courage!

What's a heart's favorite dance? The heartbeat boogie!

Why did the heart decorate the house? To spread love!

What's a heart's favorite story? A love tale!

Why do hearts love to draw? They love creating love lines!

What did the heart say to the lungs? "You take my breath away!"

Why did the heart take a picture? To capture its love!

What's a heart's favorite hobby? Sending love letters!

Why was the heart sparkling? It was full of glittery joy!

What's a heart's favorite color? Red, for love!

13.Animals Jokes

Why did the dog love Valentine's Day? It was paw-some!

What's a cat's favorite Valentine treat? Chocolate mice!

Why did the rabbit bring flowers? It was hopping with love!

What's a fish's Valentine wish? "You're fintastic!"

Why did the owl write a poem? It wanted to say "Owl always love you!"

What's a bee's favorite Valentine line? "Bee mine!"

Why did the horse write a card? It was galloping with love!

What's a pig's Valentine wish? "You're sow special!"

Why did the bird sing on Valentine's Day? It was tweeting sweet tunes!

What's a squirrel's Valentine message? "I'm nuts about you!"

Why did the lion roar on Valentine's Day? It was roaring with love!

What's a cow's Valentine line? "I love moo!"

Why did the goat bring chocolates? It wanted to bleat its heart out!

What's a penguin's favorite Valentine gift? Ice hearts!

Why did the butterfly smile? It had fluttery feelings!

What's a dog's Valentine message? "Paws and kisses!"

Why did the fox send a card? It was slyly in love!

What's a chicken's Valentine line? "You crack me up!"

Why did the zebra write a card? It was lined with love!

What's a frog's Valentine wish? "Hop on over to my heart!"

14.Friendship Jokes

Why did the peanut butter and jelly stay best friends? They were the perfect spread!

Why did the crayons love their friendship? They made life colorful!

Why did the puzzle pieces stay friends? They always fit together!

Why did the book thank its friend? They were on the same page!

Why did the cookies remain friends? They always shared the dough!

What's the best gift for a best friend on Valentine's Day? A hug that sticks!

What do friends write in Valentine's cards? "You're my BFForever!"

What's a friend's favorite Valentine gift? Time together!

What's the sweetest thing a friend can say? "You're a real treasure!"

What's a friend's favorite Valentine line? "You're my partner-in-crime!"

Why do friends love Valentine's Day? It's an excuse to celebrate each other!

What's a best friend's favorite emoji? 😊!

Why did the kite love its buddy? They lifted each other up!

What do pencils say on Valentine's Day? "We're better together!"

Why did the heart share chocolate? Sharing is caring!

What do friends love about Valentine's Day? It's all about connection!

Why did the puzzle say thank you? It found its missing piece in a friend!

What's a loyal friend's Valentine message? "Always by your side!"

Why do best friends never miss Valentine's Day? It's another reason to smile!

What do stars say to friends? "You light up my sky!"

15.Nature Jokes

Why did the tree fall in love? It found its roots in someone special!

What's a flower's favorite Valentine's song? "Blossom in Love!"

Why did the cloud send hearts? To shower love!

What's a leaf's Valentine message? "You're unbe-leaf-able!"

Why did the sun smile? It was beaming with love!

What's a snowflake's Valentine wish? "You're snow special!"

Why did the river write a Valentine? It wanted to flow with love!

What do mountains say on Valentine's Day? "I'm rock-solid for you!"

Why do roses always get love letters? They're the symbols of love!

What's a tree's favorite Valentine's card? Something sappy!

Why did the garden feel special? It was blooming with love!

What's the moon's Valentine message? "You're out of this world!"

Why did the ocean blush? It saw its reflection in love!

What's a butterfly's Valentine wish? "You give me

Why do bees love Valentine's Day? They're sweet on everyone!

What's the earth's favorite Valentine gift? A bouquet of flowers!

Why did the rainbow smile? It was spreading colorful love!

What do forests do on Valentine's Day? They branch out to spread joy!

Why did the star write a love note? It wanted to twinkle in someone's life!

What's a tree's favorite Valentine's line? "You're tree-mendous!"

16.Funny Kids' Jokes

Why did the skeleton skip Valentine's Day? It didn't have the guts to ask someone out!

What's a vampire's favorite Valentine candy? Fang-tastic fudge!

Why did the cookie cross the road? To get to its sweet-heart!

What do you call two ducks in love? Quack-mates!

Why did the frog fall in love? It met its prince!

What's a robot's favorite Valentine gift? A byte of love!

Why did the giraffe get a Valentine? It had a tall order of love!

What's a witch's favorite Valentine potion? Love at first spell!

Why do chickens celebrate Valentine's Day? Because they egg-spect love!

What did the puppy say to the kitten? "Paw-lease be my Valentine!"

Why did the astronaut send chocolates? It was over the moon in love!

What's a detective's Valentine wish? "Let's solve the case of love!"

Why did the dinosaur write a Valentine? It wanted to roar with love!

What's a pirate's Valentine message? "You're my trea-sure!"

Why did the pencil blush? It got drawn to someone!

What's a kangaroo's Valentine wish? "Hop into my heart!"

Why did the turtle fall in love? It was a slow and steady kind of love!

What's a hedgehog's Valentine's Day card? "You're sharp and sweet!"

Why did the horse write a song? To gallop into someone's heart!

What's a unicorn's Valentine gift? A magical kiss!

17.Sports Jokes

Why did the soccer ball fall in love? It was kicked into someone's heart!

What's a tennis player's Valentine wish? "Love all!"

Why did the basketball team celebrate Valentine's Day? They wanted to score big on love!

What's a runner's favorite Valentine line? "You make my heart race!"

Why did the golfer send chocolates? It was a hole-in-one kind of love!

What's a bowler's favorite Valentine gift? A perfect strike of love!

Why did the baseball player write a poem? To pitch their heart!

What's a swimmer's favorite Valentine line? "You're making waves in my heart!"

Why did the skater fall for Valentine's Day? It was a smooth ride to love!

What's Cupid's favorite sport? Archery!

Why did the football player bring roses? To tackle someone's heart!

What's a gymnast's Valentine's Day message? "You flip my heart!"

Why do track stars love Valentine's Day? It's a sprint to someone's heart!

What's a skier's favorite Valentine gift? A snow-kiss!

Why did the coach love Valentine's Day? It's a game plan for love!

What do you call a hockey player in love? A "goal-mate!"

Why did the bike rider celebrate Valentine's Day? They were on the road to love!

What's a volleyball player's favorite Valentine line? "You've set my heart!"

Why did the marathon runner propose? They went the extra mile for love!

What's a boxer's Valentine wish? "Let's fight for love together!"

18.Technology Jokes

Why did the computer go on a date? It wanted to find its match online!

What's a keyboard's favorite Valentine line? "You're just my type!"

Why did the mouse bring chocolates? It clicked with someone special!

What do Wi-Fi routers give on Valentine's Day? A strong connection!

Why did the smartphone write a poem? To dial into someone's heart!

What's an email's Valentine wish? "You've got mail... of love!"

Why did the printer blush? It got jammed with feelings!

What do headphones say to their Valentine? "I'm all ears for you!"

Why did the hard drive propose? It couldn't store its feelings any longer!

What's a selfie's favorite Valentine line? "Picture us together!"

Why did the charger and phone fall in love? They completed each other!

What's a tablet's Valentine gift? A screen full of hearts!

Why did the app send a message? It wanted to notify its crush!

What's a computer's favorite Valentine activity? Logging into love!

Why did the camera blush? It captured too much love!

What's a drone's Valentine wish? "I'm hovering for you!"

Why did the smartwatch write a Valentine? To tell someone they're on time for love!

What's a robot's favorite Valentine gift? A programmed hug!

Why did the calculator fall in love? It counted on someone special!

What's an emoji's favorite Valentine line? "Heart eyes for you!"

19. Music Jokes

Why did the musician send a Valentine? To hit the right note!

What's a guitar's favorite love song? "You pluck my heartstrings!"

Why did the drum join the Valentine's Day party? It wanted to beat with love!

What's a singer's favorite Valentine gift? A duet of love!

Why did the piano write a Valentine? It was keyed into someone special!

What's a DJ's Valentine wish? "You spin me right round!"

Why did the violin fall in love? It was played by Cupid's bow!

What's a trumpet's favorite Valentine line? "You blow me away!"

Why did the microphone get chocolates? It had a lot to amplify about love!

What's a songwriter's Valentine card? Lyrics straight from the heart!

Why did the orchestra celebrate Valentine's Day? They were in harmony with love!

What's a saxophone's favorite love song? "You're so smooth!"

Why did the flutist blush? It couldn't handle all the sweet notes!

What's a drummer's Valentine's Day message? "You keep my heart in rhythm!"

Why did the headphones fall in love? They wanted to tune into someone's heart!

What's a singer's favorite Valentine card? A love note!

Why did the harp propose? It had all the right chords!

What's a rock star's Valentine's wish? "You rock my world!"

Why did the metronome fall in love? It kept perfect time!

What's a choir's favorite Valentine song? "All You Need is Love!"

20.Magical Valentine's Day Jokes

Why did the wizard send a Valentine? To cast a spell of love!

What's a unicorn's favorite Valentine treat? A rainbow of chocolate hearts!

Why did the fairy sprinkle glitter? To add sparkle to love!

What's a mermaid's Valentine wish? "You're fintastic!"

Why did the dragon fall in love? It was burning with passion!

What's a magician's Valentine's Day message? "You've got me under your spell!"

Why did the phoenix celebrate Valentine's Day? It rose with love from the ashes!

What's a genie's Valentine wish? "You make all my dreams come true!"

Why did the elf write a Valentine? To spread magic in someone's heart!

What's a fairy's favorite Valentine gift? A kiss on the wings!

Why did the centaur send flowers? It galloped into love!

What's a witch's favorite Valentine's Day recipe? A love potion!

Why did the leprechaun bring chocolates? To share his pot of love!

What's a wizard's favorite Valentine card? A scroll full of love spells!

Why did the goblin blush? It found gold in someone's heart!

What's a giant's Valentine gift? A heart bigger than the sky!

Why did the wand sparkle on Valentine's Day? It was waving with love!

What's a Pegasus's Valentine wish? "Fly away with me!"

Why did the spellbook write a love letter? It was enchanted by someone!

What's the best Valentine gift for a sorcerer? A charm filled with love!

Wow, you made it to the end of the book! Wasn't that so much fun? I hope your heart is full of love and your cheeks are sore from laughing so much. Valentine's Day is such a special time—it's not just about candy or cards, but about making each other smile and feeling warm inside. And laughter, my friend, is one of the best ways to show love!

Think about it: every time you tell a joke from this book, you're spreading happiness. Maybe you made your best friend laugh so hard they snorted milk out of their nose. Or maybe you got your grandpa to chuckle even though he says he's heard every joke in the world. Those moments are what Valentine's Day is all about—showing people you care by making them feel happy.

So here's your next mission: pick your favorite jokes from this book and share them! Tell them to your friends at school, your family at the dinner table, or even your pet (though your dog might just tilt its head and wag its tail). You never know—you might just make someone's whole day brighter!

And don't forget, you don't have to wait for Valentine's Day to spread love and laughter. Every single day is a good day to share a joke, give a hug, or just tell someone how much they mean to you. Your smile and your kindness are gifts that the world needs, so don't be shy about sharing them.

Alright, little comedian, it's time to go out there and make the world laugh! Keep being sweet, keep being funny, and keep being YOU—because you're amazing, and the world is so much better with you in it.

Happy Valentine's Day and happy joking! 

Made in the USA
Monee, IL
07 July 2026